MOUTHY

MOUTHY

Emily Rose Kahn-Sheahan

FIRST PRINTING

Published by Thoughtcrime Press
thoughtcrimepress.com

Artwork: Patricia Sazani

Cover design by Debra Kayes
debrakayes.com

Interior layout by Josh Gaines
Typeset in Perpetua and Futura

ISBN-10: 0-9887167-2-0
ISBN-13: 978-0-9887167-2-8

Library of Congress Control Number: 2016933441

Printed on acid free paper in the United States of America

10 9 8 7 6 5 4 3 2 1

Table of Contents

The Spinster

The Mouth

Acknowledgments / 64

Mouthy

My mouth don't let me be
quiet. Got a boom throat,
trench deep marathon breath
carries my noise all the way
back to the beginning. Drum
tongue. Make the rattlesnakes
shimmy. So sharp I shave
that look off your face. Say *Big*.
I say *fit all the fathoms in my cheeks*.
You don't like these sass red lips,
want the pretty to lay quiet, stop
causing all this fuss, but I got
firecracker teeth popping.
They get me into the good
trouble worth all this voice.

THE TROUBLE

Fire Sign

Never been anywhere they didn't
try to hand me keys. I have deep
pockets and the will to never be
enough. Call me scaffold or

feather bed. I'll make myself both
if you say I can't. That's magic,
manifest proof that I, alone, can
make me small. Tell me *no* and watch

the tantrum. I buried a closet
full of red for fear it would catch
fire. That's magic. Don't look
under the bed. That's not hiding,

it's where I keep what to forget.
I bury the keys there. I make
nests of old clothes, remember
what they made me seem.

I hide to make you look. That's
magic. You never stop looking.

The Night Lonely Met Need

The first time Lonely let fingers
cross the length of her hip and dip
beneath cotton she had her back against it.
It didn't matter where the hand became

a name she can't remember. The thrill
was not knowing the direction of fingers,
a change of pressure, the unexpected
thumb. The room was full of party

yet here was this hand undercover
introducing slick to purpose and then
came shiver. Lonely's body betrayed how new
this stranger's crossing. The begging

arch of her spine reached back,
the crowded room,
the sudden emptiness.

Dirty Thought II –

Touch is a greedy sense
but he wants me to look
at him. My body hoards
breath to drive the rippling
cry through me. Pleasure
is blindfold focused.

He wants to watch the
iris retreat. Proof he's
done this and I am here
with him. This magic.
My windows flung open.

Because We Promised To Take It Slow

By some chaste phenomenon, we managed not
to fuck each other, but spent the night introducing our hands,
the easy tangle of limbs. I didn't think we would
make it when I felt your breath hitch, your body decide it was done
with polite and I wasn't going to stop you. I blame the long day
leading you to my bed, credit your mouth, and the collapse
that followed with our almost good behavior. The morning

was our reward, well-slept, despite heat cradling my body.
We passed hours in gentle mapping, folded
around each other in the deliberate simmer
of skin. Appetite bloomed in my throat when you said, I want
you to touch me. The eager giving of my mouth reward for your
not pushing, the thirsty sound of thank you
                                    thank you

                                                        thank you.

A History Of Wanting People To Look At Me

Out of context
the man walks in
I say
nothing
and finger my lips
assume he'll notice
how empty my mouth
is without him
like magic
they all look
casual
spectacle
wanton display
a child
on the dance floor
spinning
her hands wide

The Stretch

I never considered preference past
the strong veins in your forearms,
my nervous pulse and blushing foot-
shuffling response. Boys in high school
spat on my car for its equal sign, called
my large and strong and lack of interest
in their chest pounding *rug munching bitch*.
They wouldn't understand a limber geometry,
a straight line, slightly bowed. My skin
wants to bend around you and pull
your binding tight.

Dirty Thought IV: Ripe Fruit, In Season

Warm and flush, skin gives
way under your suckling lips.
Chin dripping, you worry
at my pit.

This is what Summer
smells of: salt
and effort. Heat
clings to this sticky
feast of me. I am
a selfish peach milking
your tongue, a swollen fig
opening, a body racked
with blossoming.

Cake

I baked you a cake. I know
it's not your birthday
and we don't know
each other yet but I made this
for you. I know
you're going to like it.

I put all my favorite things inside
so your tongue can learn these things
I like. I blew out the candles and made
a wish for you while I licked
the batter from my fingers. I wished

for you. Made a wish for you.
I wished for something for you.
You are something of a wish I made
while I licked the batter
from my fingers. Would you like some

of this wish I made with my fingers
and batter on my tongue? I know
it's not your birthday but I made this
batter like a wish for you. I burned
candles in my bedroom. Mixed
batter on my back and baked it
with the heat in my belly. I made

this heat for you. Burned my belly
with a wish for you. I know
you're going to like these things
I know. I made a wish and put

all my favorite things inside you.
Blew your candle into furnace flame.
I made this bedroom

out of cake for you. I know
you don't know this room but I know
you're going to like it.

I made this belly for your back to lick
with your fingers so your tongue
can learn these things I like.

I like you. Made this batter
from my heat for you. Would you
like some? I'd like to know you
like my tongue. My fingers want to know
the favorite things you like. I burned this room
like a candle for you. It's not your birthday
but make a wish for me.

I am a birthday cake
burning like a candle
for you. Our tongues don't know
each other yet. Make a wish.
Put all your favorite things inside
my belly. We'll bake each other with the heat
from our fingers. Make a bedroom from my back
and know these things I like. Let's wish furnace. Let's
make batter. Let's bake a cake together.

Knives And Flame

The waiter makes me nervous
but I keep asking questions
he is pleased to answer.

I need to drag him to the back
corner where we polish knives.
Every time he says *girlfriend*

I assume it's a reminder I shouldn't
look at him like he's a bone to clean.

The boy with the bonfire, the backyard,
is trying. He's never used charm
as trade. He's odd and obvious. I let the fire
next to him fascinate me instead.

At what point does *good* become
more exciting than watching wood
split as flame presses deep into the grain?

The Trouble With Resisting Temptation Is It May Never Come Again
Fortune Cookie

I tried to see my body as he
unwrapped it. Not the careful
inventory I take from the mirror.

Eager stranger, muttering things
of want as his hands searched
my skirt. Spanked my ass for looking
so delicious. How dare I be this body

and forget how beautiful it ripples,
the art in bountiful meat, milk skin.
Curve drunk on my own hips,
I let him deserve me.

What Lonely Won't Say

A Mexican restaurant is no place
for a married man's hands
to wander. When his left slides
up my skirt, I stop it, but wonder
if I'm slick enough for his ring
to slip inside me. Imagine the gold
rooting, the sour accomplice
stink. My tongue forked for the lies
to pass easy. *No* should be
the obvious reflex, not wrestling
with my parting knees, my eyes
unblinking, my mouth's sudden
taste for salt.

Lonely Again

My mood annoys her. She can't understand
why we're home on a Friday.
She slips on whatever's black, low cut
Where are all your friends?
lines her eyes
Where did the party go?
sharpens her teeth
Did you lose the bottle?
and blots her red lips
Why aren't we pouring it on the fire again?

She doesn't want to watch *Battlestar Galactica*.
She knows the ending.
She has my phone.
She's texting every bad idea.
She just smoked my last cigarette
and bitched about my bank account.
Feeding her gets expensive.

I try to go to bed but she
asks for water,
has to pee,
twitches next to me all night,
whines at the alarm,
insists on painting my face when we're late
again, rolls a joint and begs me
to forget. If she'll lie still, I promise

her the fire, to flay the night
and open my skin to feed her.

Where The Noise Lives

When I run out of ideas and my apartment is a funhouse
screaming distraction, I go to the bar and pray
there's no game. The clink and crowd mutter thickens
the air until my head stops spinning useless. Whiskey helps.

The bartender with a crooked mouth knows
my name, greets me with a holler and high five, his hair
mad-man greasy. He is my ally and knows my *one*
always means *three*. I don't want my mother to know

how well he knows my name, the nights I've turned myself
inside out before him. I've named each of his missing teeth.
She pictures gutters, blackouts, her own parents. I try to explain
the way art loves noise. The way my brain craves cacophony
and bars make the thickest racket. Translating this vocabulary
becomes too fitful. I stop telling her stories or substitute
"coffee" or "café" even though they both give me heartburn.

She tells me, I used to fall asleep on the floor in the middle
of her parties, afraid I'd miss something. I don't say
rows of shotglasses. I tell her *I am a top spinning and can only sleep
with the TV on* and spare her names I don't remember.
I tell her I paint my face happy and go where the noise lives
but won't confess how I spin wild sometimes, mutter *better than shut-in
and no sleep.*

She opens a bottle of wine when the dog is with her, asks
if it's still drinking alone.

THE WINTER

Salt Moon

This moon calls men who like to touch me best
when my eyes are wet. I blame her for how close
the dead are to skin on this side of the year. The pull
of hearts suffering her tide. I dive for them,
soak my skirts and carry that weight too.

This moon has a way of skinning me. I want
to heal without her moonshine pouring off
every body, calling closer, *please closer.* I blame her
for my constant asking, for the bottle, my crooked back,
all I wish to bury. I blame the moon for her restless winter.
Even in my sleep, she winks as she wanes
but stares wide at me.

Lonely Locks The Doors

Lonely cleans the kitchen five times
this week. Hasn't done laundry
in months and the room smells
like a feral nest, but Lonely

calls it sanctuary, reliable
and vaults it shut. Lonely
dreams another body better
than this always skin and tries to
stay sleeping. Lonely cries best
in cars so Lonely stops

going places, stops dressing. The shower
too similar to caring, Lonely turns the skin
inside out. These are secrets Lonely keeps

from spilling out where everyone can see. Lonely
always keeps the kitchen clean.

Pretty Lies

I was a genius before I knew
to try. Haphazard prodigy.
Immaculate accident. Just by breathing
a new type of sigh. I'll try to make it
seem more tragic: I'm alone,

always have been. So many
histories more torn and tattered
and ruined and rising from the rubble
than this sad sack. Suppose I said,
the last piece of paper on earth

and I used it to draw a cat. I stole my mouth
from a woman with a better story. Tell me
it's the best lie I ever believed.

Colossus

I picture myself a mighty
titan. My heart swallows
me in bits, the way I pick
at scabs and scratch
my skin raw. It starts as relief,
turns sinister. I drink the desert
and call it waterfall. My body
grows so large I am endless
consuming, a glutton
for my own blood. Take it.
I have enough to spare.

The Time We All Gave Up Sex

I wasn't having any anyway.
It was an easy bet. Caviar
for lent. We started buying more
whiskey. It was winter anyway.
The moon made our skin hum.
The amaryllis grew two feet
and flowered all season
from the tension. We played spades
instead. Drank the shit-talk and bought
a bigger couch. I gave up nothing
really. I just stopped trying.
I wasn't trying anyway. I think
we gave up trying. It wasn't hard
to let go. I wasn't holding on anyway.
The body adapts to a fast the way it forgets
pain. When Ben gave in and Aricka's rage
needed outlet, I swallowed the moon, kept it
warm, learned to color, grew an extra tooth.

Lonely, Don't Be That Girl

Don't hate that girl crying
at the bar, a harbinger
of low tide and floodwater
balanced on the corner stool
alone on one side. Friendly

crowded on the other. It's 2am.
She shouldn't have left
the house. The first whiskey
chased the sullen. Her friends
drink enough to forget the way
she salts her whiskey.

They want to hate her
or cut her off and call her
a cab. She's a puddle

in their fray, invisible
amid the open mouths
lining the room. Her friends
can't see the fool moon
she swallowed. She chokes
on the party they try
too hard to enjoy.

Tipping Point

My mother says, *depressed.*
I respond *roller-coaster hiccup.*
Say *the world isn't round,*
remind her of waves and moon.

My body says, *exhaustion,*
creaks like a restless bed.
Every step sand bags
and rusty hinges.

My cracks are showing.
My mom wants to make sure I've noticed.
She makes me tea.

I say, *the sky stopped falling,*
thank her for believing me.
She worries into the steam
and wishes I cried more.

Dirty Thought VI: Kiss Me

I mean I want a piece of you
in my mouth, need to taste
the intention, the flavor
of your body flexed.

I mean tell me
how you screw.
Listen and lead
the exchange of give
and teeth and tongue
and lip and waltz.
I mean dance with me.
I mean fuck me.
I mean feed me

your mouth like hunger
wet and driving. Hum
into my throat
like it's the last song
you'll ever sing, forget
your lyrics on the tip
of my tongue.

I mean play my favorite
game of tag. Show me
the mud you like
roll around in it.
Choose your lip.
Tell me switch
and flip. Listen
for the yes I lick
along your teeth. Say
chase, say take, say choke.

I mean come with me.
I mean, it's ok
to cum now. I mean wait,
cum now. I mean we're
not going to fuck
tonight. I mean kiss me
until I regret it.

Whiskey Tongue To Lonely
After Rachel McKibbens

It's okay to spread wide. Your lock is rusted
obsolete and foolish anyway. You can run wild now.

The clock in your bones chimes hard. Take its humming
impulse and wander into the rich night. It's okay to frequent

dark corners. Light them with the hot welcome of your lips.
Hunger means more than wine and fresh batteries.

It's okay to wish for sweat and chase the skin slap
of friendly hips. It's okay to bay like a bitch in heat. Bent back

and howling like the animal itching beneath your skin.
There is another type of power your mother

never explained. Her march is thirty one years behind your open
chest, and yes you can be as wet and wanton as your skin

whispers you should. This isn't about the sin inside.
God made your flexible squeeze for a reason. *Holy!*

Holy! It's okay to be a craven creature brightly plumed
and open. Caw and crow with your hungry throat and know

you are made with strings worth plucking. The music of your
body is a midnight gospel singing *Amen!*

THE SPINSTER

36 Questions

They say there are 36 questions
we can ask each other. Like
frogs who refuse to leap
from water before it boils,
we'll fall in love before we notice
the danger. Every pot of standing water
looks sinister. Boiling is in my top five
fears of dying. Fire and hot oil
also make the list. Alone
sits at the top.

36 Answers

1. I want to have dinner with my great-grandmothers
2. and to never be famous.
3. I have conversations with you in my head. In my head I'm as bold as everyone thinks.
4. It rains a little on every perfect day.
5. I sing to myself when things go well and when I want attention. I'll never sing happy birthday to you on your birthday.
6. If I live to ninety before I lose my mind, I'll die as soon as holes appear. Betty taught me that grace.
7. Smoking will kill me.
8. We both need to be alone, love a front stoop and offer our skin as generosity.
9. I never feel incapable
10. but I wish they'd given me Ritalin earlier.
11. I used to tell my life story to strangers in three minutes for high scores.
12. I want to wake knowing how to make music
13. and ask a crystal ball if I should give up on children.
14. I dream of breathing underwater, going to balls and wearing corsets. Things I can't, haven't, and already have.
15. I've never accomplished anything I'd call the greatest ever. I never plan to settle for one.
16. My friends are good witches and complicated people.
17. I treasure the memory of my grandmother's last birthday
18. and try not to think about tilt-a-whirls.
19. I would never stop kissing you.
20. Everything I want in a partner except sex.
21. I always prefer to touch. I love with my hands. My magic lives there too.
22. You go first.
23. My family is more warm than close. I am grateful my childhood wasn't worse.
24. Blessed and easily frustrated.
25. I can't answer this alone.
26. The whole truth.

27. I have less confidence than bluster.
28. I try my best to terrify you. You refuse to run.
29. I accidentally shit my pants three different times.
30. I wept over a boy I barely liked because he didn't want me.
31. You like me.
32. Betrayal and abuse.
33. I love/forgive you. I'm sorry.
34. When my neighbors' garage caught fire, I took a picture
    of my grandmother, my computer, my phone, my charger. A memory,
    all my poems, a way to call for help.
35. Any of the children, but my mother's death will skin me.
36. I have to undo my locks to love you. Behind the metal, I am meat.
    Do I seem nervous staring at your teeth?

The Problem With Tarot And Online Dating

I draw three cards because I believe the fortune
has more weight than what I accomplish
in an afternoon. The ship is sinking or I am juggling
a hand holding the cup I will refill now.
Whiskey and root beer or communion or whatever
you call Tuesday.

A random playlist skirts the memory of
each song's introduction: The 1970 Buick with a sofa
for a backseat, the fifth hour of a long drive
alone, my father's tape deck. Play me all the songs
that mean nothing yet. I'll try and seem gracious.

It matters. If I had your phone number I'd send you
drunk texts, but only on weekdays. By which I mean
I'd make a great housewife. Fingers in every pot
domesticated. Dick in my mouth and happy on a Tuesday
for no particular reason other than I am your wife. Happy
unable to scare us. Maybe even some chickens in the backyard

I'd kill to feed you. Call us a garden and leave your shoes
on the front porch. I draw three cards because I don't want
to call my brother. I don't want to talk about our father.
Let's play a game where you ask me a question.

My answer is amazing and forever is a foregone Tuesday.
The sun is barely set and you don't even know
I have two last names already. So many secrets
I'm going to whisper. You'll swallow them all
and teach me gracious.

Lonely Runs Backwards

Lonely says she lets them leave.
She left with no hint or sorry goodbye.
Lonely left quick because he kept looking. Lingered.
He would have left. You'd never guess
Lonely so nimble. Runs like a liar.

Have You Considered Freezing Your Eggs?

This is my slow winter, my constant, the bloom
that won't bud in frost, unseasoned.
I've made this home, the empty terrain,
cultivated strength inside a vacancy.

I was made with urgency only to accomplish.
Great acres of potential. Scramble for the trees
to bury pockets full of complaints. Forget
the rush to bare before barren settles.

Forget the constant of aging, the years
burn page after empty page. Forget
the fire's slow smolder, the wrecking
measure. I am not old, not even barely
worried until she asks.

—

Chicago, October

I should ignore how the empty city in my gut
still billboards your name. Twice
I've asked you to leave and kept the door
open. I couldn't stand the sound of a lock
clicking a steadfast *no*, when we
have always been *maybe*.

I fall for your open *hello* every time.
You ghost *one day* through my chest
and my foolish city believes you.
Last night I chased the back of your head
through a crowded room and woke
with hands clenched, legs wide
and reaching.

When my mind wanders and he asks
what I am thinking, I never
say your name, never admit
my nipples firm at the thought
of your plucking fingers. I say
Kiss me, occupy myself
with his open lips and swallow
your taste.

Sometimes, he carries her ghost
to bed with us. His hands trace
the length and curve of me
to assure himself that this is not
her body. When I ask
what he's thinking, he nibbles
the places I've shown him, my places,
until I am clutch and shiver.

When we fuck, sometimes you and she
get tangled in our sheets. We do our best
not to draw attention to you. We fuck
harder. I know this rhythm belongs
to him and her hips were never
as hungry as mine. This
is how we choose to fill
the cleft of your names.

The Two Men I Was In Love At

I would have poured myself into them
knowing their colander ways.

I'm grateful for how each dammed
themselves against the deluge

I suppose. I fear drowning more
than breaking but my open doors

still whisper *fools* when I say I am happy
for them. I never got to strip them to skin

on some floor and bring the house down
around our bucking. I would have slipped

my taste into everything they craved
until my name meant hunger. It's easy

to say I was too much fire for them
when I have nothing but wet matches

and the need for heat. If I could go back
I'd be the same.

When my mother asks, "Have you considered dating women?"

It's not that the topography
is unappealing,
or that women aren't
more attractive
company. I wonder
how much I choose
and how much is rigid
habit of the body. I never
called it *wrong,* thought
I'd tried. I was 19
and kissing Mary
and I never pictured her body.
Maybe I never pictured
my body. In dreams
of naked women, I become
a man. I say, *Yes.*

Dirty Thought III: His Content

In my mouth he is new honey
suckled. Eager, sweat not sweet.
The muscled supple of his most
naked, my favorite flex.
A blood full reflection
of me under his skin. His thick
was made for this wet wrapping
and I want to take it all
slow until I know every slip
and edge, the instruction
in every hip buck and roll,
until I am full and spilling
his urgent content.

Lonely Plays With Mirrors

Lonely runs head-first
into silence, fruit fly hovers,
vulture pecks the carrion
of maybe not that interested.
Lonely wears a party dress
to breakfast and makes the room
twitch, a walking yes.

Lonely opens the door over and over
though no one is asking to come in.
Prove Lonely right, that Lonely is,
has always been, will always be
an awful magician, conjuring
the same thing every time.

Accordion Song, Dawn

He sings along in Spanish, sings
to me. We're tucked beneath red sheets
somewhere close to dawn. *Corazón.*
I know this word, but I ask him
to translate, just to hear the whispered
rasp of *heart* and *lovers* and *gardenia.*

He puts on an accordion tango, says
too many think it a comedic
instrument, don't appreciate the breathing,
the complex keys to finger. He grips
my hip with his left while his right hand
nimbly plays until my breath

sings its rasp for him. I want to ask him
about boxing, but not because I care.
I like to watch his eyes go wild, his body
a pantomime of survival and skill. I don't
tell him I want to be fucked exhausted

like a fighter who refuses to drop their hands.
I don't say I feel caught with my hands down.
I tell him I want him to teach me how to dance.
When he says he needs to learn how to lead, I don't

tell him he's wrong. He flips, pulls and rocks
his wanting rhythm into my hips. We dance
all morning under those red sheets. My body
shivers in interludes between the tango
of his fingers. I dream accordions when I drift.
No bell rung. There are rounds left to fight.
Corazón. I'm not done dancing.

Lonely Explains

I can't convince the body it isn't hollow. Can't tell
the wishing heart its chambers are already full
of pennies. Every birthday candle, eyelash
and meteor shower have passed

with the same wish since I was

twelve. I don't know how

to teach the hungry

meat to eat

itself.

THE MOUTH

Lonely Picks A New Name

My body is rooted

You've noticed my clever too

I sharpen my tongue so you can hear the edge song

Pierce your ears with it and find some nice hoops

I'm mythological

Rockbiter daughter of rage and well water

They say my hands are holy

See things the way raccoons do: in terms of want

I'm hungry

I've seen 1,000 trees down today and not a single saw tooth

I want lumberjack for dinner

Trees are so definite until wind makes them worry

When pushed to sway I've heard my roots creak

Terrified to think I believe my own telling

I see standing water contain everything above

Wonder if it believes its own name

Creationism

On the 1st day
I was happy accidents,
random confluences, an act in an apartment
at the end of a blink.

By the 2nd day
I'd taught everything its name,
molded enthusiasm from dirt and heights.

Day 3
was for uneven details of the body.
I whispered

and the 4th day was Chaos.
Thus came float and brace,
swallow then bellow.

On the 5th
I added weight to the work, brought forth
buttress, brick, and blood mortar.

And on the 6th day
I called in sick, drank champagne
and ate steak for breakfast.

Through the feast I chewed on light,
spat out the universe.

If This Means Nothing, Please Say So

Who brings soup to a poker game?
My bag dripping barley on the felt.
I wear top hats to tea parties, forget
to duck in the foyer and call it
a mud room. I wore my white girl

to a BBQ. Left with sauce in my hair,
lips smeared with smoke and pig
in my teeth. The job is a reason to drink
tea and take over, the conversations
limited, comic strip easy.

My mouth maybe duct tape useful, but not
the solution to my mother problem. I think
about joints in the shower, the swell
of my right knee and the 90 degree
pinky my grandmother passes down,

wonder if she'd sell that too or shove it
into my pocket with the rest of her
scarves and grapefruit spoons. She
brings caviar to the dog fight and talks
about how dirty the floors are,

wonders if her bedroom is too green
now that my mother's are honeydew.
I leave my walls taupe. We keep
our wood floors and buy more socks
than we'll ever have feet. I stole

a lighter from Walgreen's
when the clerk was rude to the black
woman's kids. Seemed right to hide it
in my palm and pay for the milk. I'm not
supposed to have dairy, but cigarettes

are still okay. My favorite word this week is
asinine. I went to a birthday and stole
the party outside, dropped it in the fire pit.
I left without my coat. I never paid the cover.
I go to the bar with an empty

wallet and a purse lined with rice crackers,
a bruised apple and I'm still awful
at Scrabble and due dates. I never read
your book or I read that one poem, just
that last line and then watched two seasons

of Buffy and didn't shower for three days.
I found your book in my laundry
basket where I hoped to find clean underwear.
I don't feel like apologizing.
I ate all the cereal. I feel worse

about ruining the poker table, pooping
in the hotel room bathroom while the other girls
were sleeping. I only shit when it will go quickly.
I only made soup once, redeemed it with bacon.
I wish everything were that easy.

Dirty Thought V: What I Do Want To Talk About

I didn't say *dungeon.*
Say *silk,* used rough
don't panic. I am strong.
It's hard to always *can do.*

You do for me. Take
this strong and pull it
hard. Now. I want you

to pull harder, take it
from me. Silk used
a little rough. Say
strong. You can take
strong from me,

for me. It's hard
to let go, not
panic. Take this
strong. Hold it. Down
tight. Now.

Song Of The Helpful

I'd rather be talking about sex. Lord knows
I like a heavy masculine, some mutual writhe
and sticky consent, but there is too much
rise and tread on my spine. Give me your hand,

I'll help you climb. I pick the fruit ready to fall.
Rescue the soft and bruised, carry it
in my hungry skirt, haven't eaten a bite.
I gorge on the still life's promise of action, watch
rotten fruit flower with no love for soil

that bore its kicking roots. Beneath the thick
I am full of soft spots. I nurse my slights,
lick my pride and tuck myself back into shadow.

We are not supposed to shine. We
hold lights, reflect sun and illuminate
a blooming great. *Bitch* and *Bitter*

ground by our teeth, rolled between
tongue and cheek. No one wants to hear
this voice ugly with protest. Be pretty, quiet, helpful,
bend your back and raise these boys high
with your forklift heart. Be workhorse prancing
complacent gaits, bridled, broken, and constant.

Permission

I may ask you to fuck me in a church. I'm sorry
if this makes you uncomfortable, but *god* never comes
easily to my lips without ritual. Forget the bra burners
who told you to rein your dominance.

Thrust *patriarch* and *Neanderthal* into my permission
until I am *yes* and *more* and *faster* and *holy holy.* Twisting
my hair into ropes, you are honorable. I nurse the welt
of handprint-bruised thighs and am everything my mother
taught me to be, my pride wet and puddled around my ankles.

David introduced me to day-rates and commands
in unlit hotel bathrooms. I wasn't too strong for Sean
to toss me across his sheets like something disposable.
Mary showed me how a bit of force around my wrists
made me bend rules I believed were stone.

I will never tell my mother why I keep ropes in the drawer
by my bed, why I split the check before I go down on strangers.
She doesn't want to know that sometimes I dream of rape
and wake up wet. Hold me down. I won't fight you. I've asked you here
to be this for me, love me in this taking. Each gasping breath

is a gratitude. I was never glass. I am brick, blood mixed in the mortar.
Defy your mother, be brute and club. Hammer at this stone until I crack
beneath you. Bind my hands, keep me from controlling this.
I am bedrock and pillar. Remind me how to be sea.

Opening

At the end of the hallway a door
glows green or angry or locked,
jammed shut by what's behind.

Some doors get to stay shut. Some things
don't need to be revealed today,

I may tell you tomorrow.
There is a broom
I will never tell you about, a mountain
I threw away, ashes I keep
in a can under the bed.
Close the door. I'm not interested

in feelings today. This can be the first time I let
you down. *I'm sorry* is a hiccup. I'll hold
my breath now, try to swallow the room.

I've been handed a lot of keys
I never asked for. This is your door.
Sometimes I forget things.
Keys made holes in these pockets

and my mother never taught me to sew, only
to carry things. The best way
to keep a secret is to forget it.

Acknowledgments

These poems, or versions of these poems, originally appeared in:

"Fire Sign," and "Salt Moon"
After Hours Press

"Cake," and "The Problem With Tarot And Online Dating"
TriQuarterly Review

"What Lonely Won't Say"
Muzzle Magazine

"Pretty Lies," and "The Time We All Gave Up Sex"
decomP magazine

"Tipping Point"
Columbia Poetry Review

"Whiskey Tongue To Lonely"
AFFILIA

"Chicago, October," "If This Means Nothing, Please Say So," and "Song Of The Helpful"
Compose Journal

"Opening"
Jet Fuel Review

Gratitudes

To my family who always believed I should be writing and performing. Without their steadfast support, I probably would have been some other woman who occasionally wrote erotica or fan-fiction. To my mother, my writing buddy, sponsor and biggest fan who enrolled me in my first poetry workshop. To my sister who made sure I was always fed and still sends me job postings. To my brother who loves me, even if he thinks I'm not funny. To my father who is always proud of me. To my step-mother who reads all my books before my father and steers him around the dirty ones. To my grandmother who would have loved all the dirty ones best.

To my housefamily: wife Aricka Foreman, husband Ben Clark, and bestest friend Miquela Cruz, for keeping me sane and laughing. You are the best loves and the kindest witnesses. I cannot express enough love and gratitude for you. You see me in every complicated moment, becoming, recovering, collapsing and rising, but love me just the same.

To the women I circle around me: Marty McConnell, Mariah Neuroth, Kim Tilford, Maya Marshall, Stacy Fox, Katherine Winters, and Missy Hughes. You give me roots, permission, and the courage to be bold and vulnerable around every turn.

Rachel McKibbens and her entire family for becoming my family, my refuge, my heart.

Patricia Smith for her grace, genius, generosity and loving direction.

All of Real Talk Avenue, and Vox Ferus where I gestated and raised my poet-self along with most of these poems. Special thank you to Stevie Edwards for her brilliance, editorial eye, and her humbling words.

My Poetry Aunties: Jackie Langetieg, Alice D'Alessio, and Jude Genereaux. My Poetry Uncles Charlie Rossiter and Ralph Murre. Who were there at the beginning, pushing, holding and walking beside me.

Susan O'Leary and Al DeGenova, my first poetry teachers. The first to see this book as it formed. I am forever grateful. To Norbert Blei and his Cross+Roads Press who started everything by giving a 19-year-old girl a reading list, confidence, and her first ISBN#. I would not be a poet today if not for him.

Patricia Sazani for turning my mouth into art. Debra Kayes for her commitment to making my pile of mouths beautiful.

Josh Gaines, Chelsea Fiddyment and Thoughtcrime Press for giving this book such a gracious home.

Marc Smith for Slam Poetry and changing my life.

OKCupid.com, Tinder and Match.com: Thanks for nothing.

Emily Rose Kahn-Sheahan lives in Chicago where she has hosted and curated live lit shows and poetry slams for ten years. Her work has recently appeared in Columbia Poetry Review, TriQuarterly, Muzzle Magazine, decomP, After Hours, and TimeOut Chicago. Her first collection, *Cigarette Love Songs and Nicotine Kisses*, was published by Cross+Roads Press.

THOUGHTCRIME **PRESS** gathers the most important voices in writing and sculpts exceptional books around them. We are artists and craftsmen who believe in paying our authors first and more while offering our readers affordable, beautiful literary art objects.

Our authors are the press.

Our readers are the press.

We've been looking for you.

We've found you.

Join us at thoughtcrimepress.com

CPSIA information can be obtained
at www.ICGtesting.com
Printed in the USA
FSOW01n1119150316
17940FS